Beetle

Karen Hartley,
Chris Macro,
and Philip Taylor

Heinemann Library
Chicago, Illinois

Designed by Ron Kamen
Illustrated by Alan Fraser at Pennant Illustrations
Originated by Ambassador Litho
Printed in China by South China Printing Co. Ltd.

04 03 02 01
10 9 8 7 6 5 4 3 2

Library of Congress Cataloging-in-Publication Data
Hartley, Karen, 1949-
    Beetle / Karen Hartley, Chris Macro, Philip Taylor.
        p. cm. -- (Bug books)
    Includes Bibliographical references (p.) and index.
    Summary: A simple intruduction to the physical characteristics, diet, life cycle, predators, habitat, and lifespan of beetles.
    ISBN 1-57572-546-0 (lib.bdg.)
    1. Beetles--Juvenile literature. [1. Beetles.] I. Macro, Chris, 1940- II. Taylor, Philip, 1949- III. Title. IV. Series.

QL576.2.H38 2000
595.76--dc21   99-057444

Acknowledgments

The Publishers would like to thank the following for permission to reproduce photographs:

Ardea London/Pascal Goetgheluck, pp. 4, 24; NHPA/Bruce Beehler, p. 5; NHPA/G.J. Cambridge, p. 6; Bruce Coleman/Dr. Frieder Sauer, p. 7; Bruce Coleman/Andrew Purcell, p. 8; Ardea London/Bob Gibbons, p. 9; Oxford Scientific Films/G.I. Bernard, pp.10, 11, 12; Oxford Scientific Films/ Paul Franklin, p. 13; NHPA/Stephen Dalton, pp.14, 21; Oxford Scientific Films/Stephen Dalton, p. 15; Oxford Scientific Films/M. Deeble & V. Stone, p.16; Heather Angel, p. 17; Oxford Scientific Films/Doug Allan, p. 18; Bruce Coleman/Jeff Foott, p. 19; NHPA/John Shaw, p. 20; Bruce Coleman/P. Kaya, p. 22; Oxford Scientific Films/George K. Bryce, p. 23; NHPA/Anthony Bannister, p. 25; Ardea London/J.L. Mason, p. 26; Garden Matters/Colin Milkins, p. 27; Bubbles/Steve Shot, p. 28; Garden Matters, p. 29.

Cover photograph reproduced with permission of Stan Osolonski/Oxford Scientific Films.

Every effort has been made to contact copyright holders of any material reproduced in this book. Any omissions will be rectified in subsequent printings if notice is given to the Publisher.

Some words are shown in bold, **like this.** You can find out what they mean by looking in the glossary.

Contents

What Are Beetles?

Beetles are **insects**. They have six legs and two pairs of wings. There are thousands of different types of beetles.

Beetles can be found in many different sizes, shapes, and colors. The weevil in this picture is one kind of beetle. **Ladybugs** are also beetles.

What Beetles Look Like

Beetles have very hard skins. Most beetles have four wings. Two are very tough. They fold over the **transparent** flying wings to protect them.

Beetles have two **antennae** on their heads. Their large eyes are actually many small eyes side by side. Most beetles are black, brown, or dark red.

How Big Are Beetles?

One of the largest beetles is called the
Goliath beetle. It can be as large as a
man's fist. It weighs about as much as
a small apple.

Most beetles are about as big as your
thumbnail, but the smallest are very
tiny. They are smaller than the period
at the end of this sentence.

How Beetles Are Born

Some beetles are born in spring. Other types are born in autumn. Most female beetles lay many eggs. The eggs can be laid on the ground, on leaves, or in holes in the ground.

Some females guard the eggs until they
hatch. When the eggs hatch, **larvae**
crawl out. Most larvae have six legs,
but weevil larvae do not have any legs.

How Beetles Grow

Beetle **larvae** eat as much food as they can. When they have grown too large for their skins, they **molt**. The old skin breaks, and the larva wriggles out. The larva molts about three times.

Next, it becomes a **pupa**. During this period, it grows wings and changes slowly into an **adult**. Many types of beetles spend this stage underground.

What Beetles Eat

Many beetles eat other **insects**, worms, or snails. Some kill animals, and others eat animals that are already dead. Some types of beetles eat plants or seeds.

Many beetles have large jaws with **mandibles** for gripping their food. Beetle **larvae** can be very fierce. Water beetle larvae can even eat **tadpoles**.

Which Animals Eat Beetles?

Birds, lizards, and frogs eat beetles. Spiders cannot eat beetles because of their hard skins. Some beetles make noises to frighten their enemies away.

If the bloody-nosed beetle is attacked, it squirts red liquid out of its mouth to help it to escape. In some countries, people hunt some types of large beetles and make them into soup.

Where Beetles Live

There are beetles living in nearly every country on Earth. Some types live in grassland, some in woodland, and some near the edges of rivers and streams.

Some types of beetles can be found at the seashore, and others near the tops of the highest mountains. Some even share the nests of other **insects**.

How Beetles Move

Some beetles can run fast. They have long, thin legs. Other beetles have shorter, stronger legs for digging. Climbing beetles have claws or sticky pads on their feet for gripping.

Many beetles can fly, but they do not fly for long. It has to be warm for many of them to fly at all. Some have wings that are not strong enough for flying.

How Long Beetles Live

Beetles usually live for less than a year. Some are born in autumn and **hibernate** during the winter as a **larva** or **pupa**. After they have laid their eggs in spring, they die.

Other beetles born in the autumn bury themselves in the ground or under the bark of trees. They sleep through the winter as **adults**.

What Beetles Do

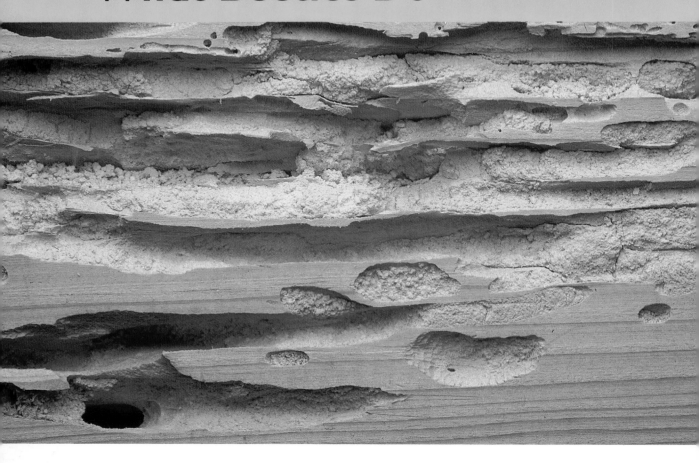

Many beetles spend their time under stones and logs. It is usually damp there and does not get too hot. Some live in people's houses, where the **larvae** cause damage by eating the wood.

Some beetles bury themselves in sand or clay. **Dung** beetles collect the dung from bigger animals. They roll it away in balls and lay an egg in each.

How Are Beetles Special?

There are more different kinds of beetles than any other type of animal. There are even beetles with legs like paddles. They live in ponds.

Some special beetles also have other names. Glowworms are not worms, but beetles. Lightning bugs are another type of beetle. They both make chemicals which can be seen in the dark.

Thinking about Beetles

Where could you find beetles? Turn over some stones and small logs to see if any are underneath. Turn them back again carefully afterwards.

Why do you think they live there? Why is that the best place for them to be? What could happen to them if they were moved to different places?

Bug Map

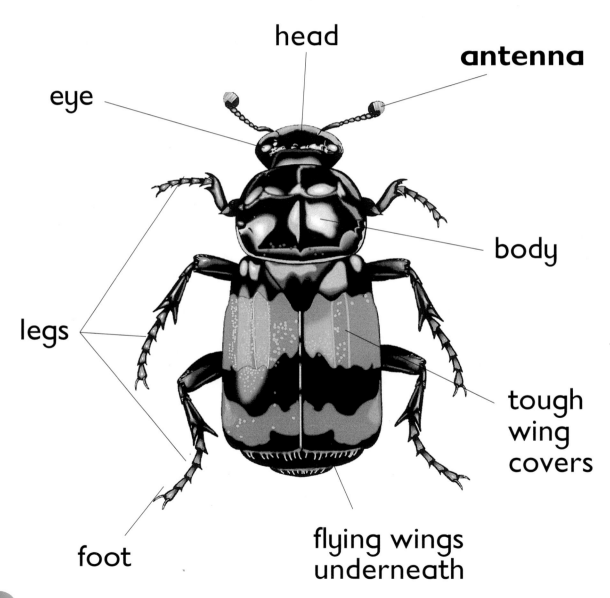

head

antenna

eye

body

legs

tough
wing
covers

foot

flying wings
underneath

Glossary

adult grown-up

antenna (more than one are antennae) thin tube on an insect's head that may be used to smell, feel, or hear

dung body waste from an animal

hatch to come out of an egg

hibernate to sleep through the winter

insect small animal with six legs

ladybug type of beetle that is usually red with black spots

larva (more than one are larvae) baby insect that hatches from an egg

mandible part of the mouth of a beetle

molt to shed an old skin that is too small

pupa (more than one are pupae) stage of an insect's life during which it turns into an adult

tadpole baby frog

transparent able to be seen through

More Books to Read

Gerholdt, James E. *Beetles*. Minneapolis: ABDO Publishing Co., 1996.

Hawcock, David. *Beetle*. New York: Random House, Inc., 1996.

Index